Contents

Some words are shown in bold, **like this**. You can find out what they mean by looking in the glossary.

Let's go south!

It is cold and windy. Snow and ice stretch out as far as the eye can see. Where is this lonely place? It is the South **Pole**, in the centre of Antarctica.

SOUTH ATLANTIC OCEAN

INDIAN OCEAN

ANTARCTICA

South Pole
+

Ross Ice Shelf

SOUTH PACIFIC OCEAN

Ross Sea

permanent ice

land

0   500   1000 miles

0   500   1000 kilometres

Explorer Tales

The South Pole

Nancy Dickmann

Raintree

www.raintreepublishers.co.uk
Visit our website to find out
more information about
Raintree books.

To order:
☎ Phone 0845 6044371
🖹 Fax +44 (0) 1865 312263
🖳 Email myorders@raintreepublishers.co.uk

Customers from outside the UK please telephone +44 1865 312262

Raintree is an imprint of Capstone Global Library
Limited, a company incorporated in England and
Wales having its registered office at 7 Pilgrim Street,
London, EC4V 6LB – Registered company number:
6695582

Text © Capstone Global Library Limited 2013
First published in hardback in 2013
Paperback edition first published in 2014
The moral rights of the proprietor have
been asserted.

Edited by Rebecca Rissman, Dan Nunn, and
    Catherine Veitch
Designed by Cynthia Della-Rovere
Levelling by Jeanne Clidas
Picture research by Elizabeth Alexander
Production by Victoria Fitzgerald
Originated by Capstone Global Library
Printed and bound in China by CTPS

ISBN 978 1 406 24193 8 (hardback)
16 15 14 13 12
10 9 8 7 6 5 4 3 2 1

ISBN 978 1 406 24200 3 (paperback)
17 16 15 14 13
10 9 8 7 6 5 4 3 2 1

British Library Cataloguing in Publication Data
Dickmann, Nancy.
The South Pole. -- (Explorer tales)
919.8'9'04-dc22
A full catalogue record for this book is available from
the British Library.

Acknowledgements
We would like to thank the following for permission to
reproduce photographs: Alamy p. 25 (© Alaska Stock);
Corbis pp. 10 (© Hulton-Deutsch Collection), 14 (©
Bettmann), 19 (© Underwood & Underwood); Getty
Images pp. 9 (Thorsten Milse), 11 (Sue Flood), 12
(Hulton Archive), 13 (Hulton Archive), 21 (Sandra Mu),
20 (Hulton Archive), 22 (Eyedea Presse), 23 (Central
Press), 27 (AFP Photo/ Guy Clavel); Photolibrary pp.
7 (BIOSPHOTO), 24; Scott Polar Research Institute,
University of Cambridge pp. 15, 18; Shutterstock pp.
5 (© Gentoo Multimedia Ltd), 6 (© Anton Balazh),
8 (© Volodymyr Goinyk), Superstock pp. 16, 29
(© Universal Images Group).

Cover photographs of Captain Roald Engelbregt
Gravning Amundsen reproduced with permission
of Superstock (© Universal Images Group); chart of
the Antarctic Polar Circle, 1703, reproduced with
permission of Sanders of Oxford, rare prints & maps
(www.sandersofoxford.com); penguins in Antarctica
reproduced with permission of Shutterstock (©
Volodymyr Goinyk). Background image of Paradise
Bay with floating iceberg, Antarctica, reproduced with
permission of Shutterstock (© Willem Tims).

Every effort has been made to contact copyright
holders of material reproduced in this book. Any
omissions will be rectified in subsequent printings if
notice is given to the publisher.

DID YOU KNOW?

The seas around Antarctica freeze solid in the winter. This is called **pack ice**, and it can trap ships.

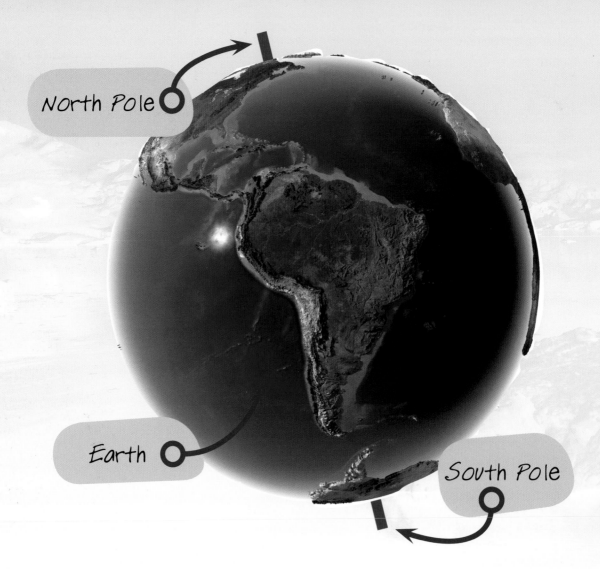

North Pole

Earth

South Pole

A **pole** is one end of an imaginary line that goes through the centre of Earth. Earth has two poles – one in the north and one in the south. At the poles, in winter the Sun never rises, and in the summer it never sets.

Exploring Antarctica

Trudging across an icy, windy landscape is hard. Dragging all your supplies along is even harder! Antarctica has very few plants, and animals live only near the coast.

DID YOU KNOW?

Many polar explorers got the disease **scurvy**. Eating fresh penguin or seal could prevent it. Yum!

Huge rivers of ice called **glaciers** move over Antarctica.

9

Early explorers

The first people to visit Antarctica were sailors hunting seals and whales. They were not interested in the South **Pole**. In the 1800s, Britain's James Clark Ross sailed near the coast of Antarctica to map it. Ross Sea was named after him.

whale

The race is on!

In 1910, a British explorer called Robert Scott sailed for Antarctica. Then he received a **telegram**. Norwegian explorer Roald Amundsen was heading for the South **Pole** as well! It would be an amazing race.

Robert Scott

Amundsen's ship, the *Fram*, was light and strong.

some of Amundsen's dogs

Amundsen started earlier, but Scott had more men. Amundsen's team skied and used dogs to pull their sledges. Scott's team pulled their sledges themselves. Who would get there first?

SCOTT'S DAILY MENU

Scott's rations included:

- pemmican (a mixture of dried meat and fat)
- biscuits
- butter
- tea
- sugar
- cocoa

Scott's men ate the same thing every day for three months!

Success and failure

Amundsen's team reached the South **Pole** first, on 14 December 1911. Scott arrived about a month later, but he had taken too long. He and his men died of cold and hunger on the way back.

Amundsen used fur clothing to keep warm and dry.

SOUTH ATLANTIC OCEAN

INDIAN OCEAN

ANTARCTICA

South Pole

- - - Scott's route
- - - Amundsen's route

Ross Ice Shelf

SOUTH PACIFIC OCEAN

Ross Sea

permanent ice

land

0   500   1000 miles

0   500   1000 kilometres

Shackleton

Irish explorer Ernest Shackleton's ship, the *Endurance*, got trapped in the **pack ice** in 1914. When the ice crushed the ship, he and his men had to abandon it. They were still 650 kilometres from land.

DID YOU KNOW?

The *Endurance* had a ship's cat, called Mrs Chippy, who killed rats and mice on board. Sadly, Mrs Chippy did not survive the trip.

Endurance

Shackleton

Shackleton's crew sailed in a tiny lifeboat for nearby Elephant Island, but they were still not safe. They had to sail another 1,300 kilometres to get help. Amazingly, everyone was rescued!

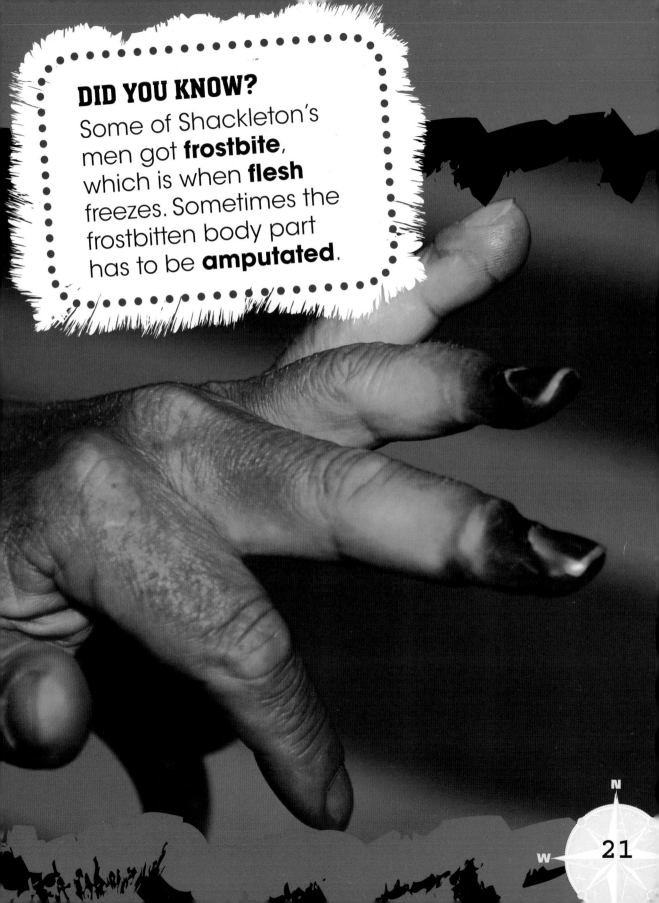

DID YOU KNOW?

Some of Shackleton's men got **frostbite**, which is when **flesh** freezes. Sometimes the frostbitten body part has to be **amputated**.

Crossing Antarctica

Shackleton had really wanted to walk across Antarctica. Ranulph Fiennes and Mike Stroud set off in 1993 to do just that. They pulled all their food and supplies on two sledges – a whopping 440 kilograms!

DID YOU KNOW?

Another explorer, called Vivian Fuchs, crossed Antarctica in 1957–1958, using motorized tractors.

Fiennes and Stroud had to work hard to pull their sledges. They did not have enough food to make up for all the energy they were using. Starving and freezing, they called a plane to rescue them.

Fiennes and Stroud had to cross the dangerous Beardmore Glacier.

The rescue plane had skis for landing on snow.

DID YOU KNOW?
On a later trip, Fiennes got **frostbite**. He **amputated** his fingers himself, in his garden shed!

The South Pole today

Today, scientists live and work at the Amundsen-Scott South **Pole** Station. The building is on stilts so it does not get buried by snow. About 50 people spend the winter here each year.

DID YOU KNOW?

Antarctica is a great place to do scientific research. Scientists there study weather, ice, rocks, fossils, stars, and how the human body deals with cold.

A scientist carries out tests on the ice.

Timeline

1839–1843   James Clark Ross maps part of Antarctica's coastline.

1911   Roald Amundsen reaches the South **Pole**.

1912   Robert Scott and his men die on the way back from the Pole.

1914   Ernest Shackleton begins his journey on the *Endurance*.

1956   The Amundsen-Scott South Pole Station is built.

1958   Vivian Fuchs completes his tractor crossing of Antarctica.

1993   Ranulph Fiennes and Mike Stroud walk across Antarctica.

Explorer's checklist

It is incredibly cold at the South Pole. Amundsen's team needed the right equipment to keep warm and travel.

goggles to prevent snow blindness (but take them off for photos!)

outer clothing and hood made of wolf skin

crampons for gripping the ice (worn when walking, not skiing)

underwear and socks made from reindeer fur

boots made of seal skin

skis and poles

grass for stuffing inside boots (it soaks up sweat)

Glossary

amputate cut off a body part because of disease or injury

crampons metal plate with spikes fixed to a boot. Crampons are used for climbing on ice or rock.

flesh muscle, fat, and skin on the surface of the body

frostbite injury caused when flesh freezes

glacier slowly moving block of ice

pack ice large pieces of floating ice

pole one end of an imaginary line that goes through the centre of Earth. Earth has a North Pole and a South Pole.

scurvy disease caused by a lack of Vitamin C. Scurvy causes tiredness, pain, and can make people's teeth fall out.

southern lights flickering lights in the night sky, caused by the Sun

telegram short message sent long distances over cables

Find out more

Books

Face to Face With Penguins, Yva Momatiuk (National Geographic Society, 2010)

Polar Animals (Saving Wildlife), Sonya Newland (Franklin Watts, 2010)

Scott of the Antarctic, Evelyn Dowdeswell, Julian Dowdeswell, and Angela Seddon (Raintree, 2012)

Who Counts the Penguins?: Working in Antarctica (Wild Work), Mary Meinking (Raintree, 2011)

Websites

www.antarctica.ac.uk/living_and_working/index.php

This is the British Antarctic Survey's website, and has information about living in Antarctica. There are also virtual tours you can take.

www.discoveringantarctica.org.uk/index.php

This website has some great videos of Antarctica.

www.spri.cam.ac.uk/resources/kids/

This website is from the Scott Polar Research Institute at Cambridge. It has lots of information and photos on Antarctica.

Index